GET WISDOM!

23 Lessons for Children

About Living for Jesus

RUTH YOUNTS

Wisdom is supreme; therefore, get wisdom!

Proverbs 4:7

© 2010 by Life*Is*Worship Publishing Group

Published by **Shepherd Press**
P. O. Box 24
Wapwallopen, PA 18660
www.shepherdpress.com
Printed in the United States of America

Page design by Tobias' Outwear for Books.

PAH 22 21 20 19 18 17 16 15 14 13 12 11 10 9 8 7 6 5 4 3 2

Contents

Introduction

A part from the gospel itself, nothing is more important to get than wisdom. It comes before education, friends, health, sports, work, and everything else you can think of. In fact, wisdom is the only good foundation for all those things.

This book illustrates qualities of wisdom and godliness. Every child of God—both adults and children—should work hard to show these traits more and more, because we love Jesus and want to be like him. That's easier said than done, isn't it? We struggle with sin every day. But thankfully, even though we often fail, we are saved by grace alone, by Christ alone! That is the GOOD NEWS. Jesus is the perfect example of all these qualities, and by his grace we can grow in wisdom and godliness.

I recommend that you memorize these verses. Talk about them every day, and don't let anything distract you or stop you from GETTING WISDOM.

> **Wisdom is supreme; therefore get wisdom.**
>   Though it cost all you have, get understanding.
> Esteem her, and she will exalt you;
>   embrace her, and she will honor you.
> She will set a garland of grace on your head
>   and present you with a crown of splendor.
>
> Listen, my son, accept what I say,
>   and the years of your life will be many.
> I guide you in the way of wisdom
>   and lead you along straight paths.
> When you walk, your steps will not be hampered;
>   when you run, you will not stumble.
> Hold on to instruction, do not let it go;
>   guard it well, for it is your life.
> Do not set foot on the path of the wicked
>   or walk in the way of evil men.
> Avoid it, do not travel on it;
>   turn from it and go on your way.
> For they cannot sleep till they do evil;
>   they are robbed of slumber till they make someone fall.
> They eat the bread of wickedness
>   and drink the wine of violence.
>
> The path of the righteous is like the first gleam of dawn,
>   shining ever brighter till the full light of day.
> But the way of the wicked is like deep darkness;
>   they do not know what makes them stumble.
>
> —Proverbs 4:7–19

Teaching Helps

This book can be used in a class or in a family. Every Christian should grow in wisdom and godliness throughout life. Parents should be helping their children acquire these traits from their earliest days. Repetition—day by day—is essential.

The Teacher's Guide, starting on **page 51,** is designed to help teach children from K-5 through Grade 4, although the lessons can easily be adapted to teach children of any age.

The Teacher's Guide provides teaching points, discussion questions, games, and role plays. Each lesson also includes a Scripture verse to help the teacher focus on the gospel, which is the starting point of all Christian character.

The questions and answers on the next page will help you explain, at a child's level, how godly character—being "good"—relates to the gospel of grace.

Christian Wisdom & the Gospel

What is Christian wisdom?

Christian wisdom is knowing and understanding the truth, obeying the truth, and making decisions based on the truth. Wisdom helps you be more like Jesus in your actions, thoughts and attitudes, by loving God and loving your neighbor.

> *Matthew 22:37-40 "'Love the Lord your God with all your heart and with all your soul and with all your mind.' This is the first and greatest commandment. And the second is like it: 'Love your neighbor as yourself.' All the Law and the Prophets hang on these two commandments."*

> *Ephesians 4:22-24 "You were taught, with regard to your former way of life, to put off your old self, which is being corrupted by its deceitful desires; to be made new in the attitude of your minds; and to put on the new self, created to be like God in true righteousness and holiness."*

Can I be good and wise—like Jesus—if I work hard enough?

No, not by yourself.

> *Romans 3:12 "There is no one who does good, not even one."*

How can I be good enough?

Only by the goodness of Jesus Christ. He was perfectly good, and he took the punishment of other peoples' sin by dying on the cross. Ask God to forgive your sin and give you a new heart. Then God will see you as though you are as good as Jesus. Also, he will help you to love and obey him.

> *Ezekiel 36:26-27 "I will give you a new heart and put a new spirit in you; I will remove from you your heart of stone and give you a heart of flesh. And I will put my Spirit in you and move you to follow my decrees and be careful to keep my laws."*

Why should I want to be good?

To show love for Jesus.

> *1 John 4:19 "We love because he first loved us."*

What do I do when it's too hard to be good?

Pray and ask God to forgive your sin. Thank him that he loves you even when you sin. Ask for God's help to practice each quality of godliness, because you love him and want to please him.

> *Phil 4:13 "I can do everything through Him who gives me strength."*

Listening

is giving careful attention to another person. Listening shows someone love and respect.

"Listen, my sons, to a father's instruction; pay attention and gain understanding."
—Proverbs 4:1

Listening is giving careful attention to another person. Listening shows someone love and respect.

EXAMPLES:

1. I should listen carefully to my homework instructions.

2. I should listen when my brother tells me about

his dream.

_____

_____

_____

_____

_____

_____

_____

PRAYER: Lord, thank you for always listening to me. It's hard for me to stop and listen to others. Usually, I want to do the talking! Please help me love others and put them first by being a good listener. In Jesus' name, Amen.

The rabbit's big ears help him listen carefully. You should listen like a rabbit!

Obedience

is doing exactly what I am asked to do, right away, with a willing attitude.

"Children, obey your parents in everything, for this pleases the Lord."
—Colossians 3:20

Obedience is doing exactly what I am asked to do, right away, with a willing attitude.

EXAMPLES:

1. When my mom calls me I should answer right away.

2. I should turn off the TV right away, without

complaining, as soon as my parents tell me to.

PRAYER: Lord, help me to obey my parents. It's too hard for me to do by myself. Thank you that you obeyed your Father perfectly, so I could be forgiven for my sin. Please give me the help I need to obey, because I want to please you. In Jesus' name, Amen.

The boy is running to obey quickly, with a good attitude.
So should you!

Contentment

is being satisfied because God is working everything together for my good and for his glory.

"I have learned **to be** content **whatever the** circumstances."

—Philippians 4:11

Contentment is being satisfied because God is working everything together for my good and for his glory.

EXAMPLES:

1. I shouldn't complain when a play date is cancelled.

2. I should be thankful for my birthday presents even when I don't get what I wanted the most.

PRAYER: Father, you give me everything I need, and you have given me what I need most—forgiveness for my sin. Please help me to be content. Sometimes I struggle with being angry and feeling sorry for myself when I don't get what I want. Please help me to be satisfied with your love and to rest in your perfect care. In Jesus' name, Amen.

The cat is content! You should be, too.

Orderliness

is keeping things in the right place and doing things at the right time.

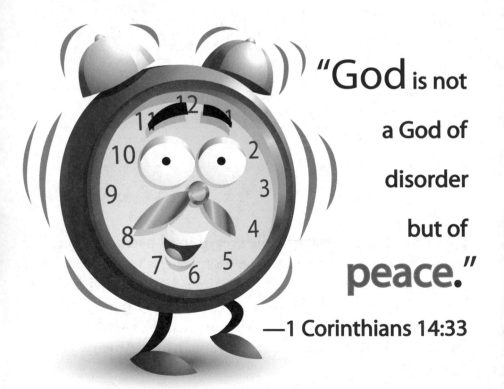

"God is not a God of disorder but of peace."

—1 Corinthians 14:33

Orderliness is keeping things in the right place and doing things at the right time.

1. I should put away my game before I go outside to play.

2. I should get up when my alarm rings.

....

....

....

....

....

....

PRAYER: Lord, thank you that you are a God of peace and order. Everything happens just the way you plan and order it. Please help me to be orderly, too. I don't always plan ahead and use my time well, or take good care of the things you've given to me. Please help me be responsible in this area. In Jesus' name, Amen.

The alarm clock reminds you to do things at the the right time!

Mercy

is showing kindness to those who are weak, sinful, and needy, because Christ loved me first when I was his enemy.

"Be kind and **compassionate** to one another, forgiving each other, just as in Christ God forgave you."
—Ephesians 4:32

Mercy is showing kindness to those who are weak, sinful, and needy, because Christ loved me first when I was his enemy.

1. When my little brother is tired and whiny, I can comfort him or play quietly with him, instead of being annoyed.

2. When my friend says something unkind, I should try to overlook it in love, remembering that sometimes I am unkind, too, even though I don't want to be.

PRAYER: Father, thank you for being merciful to me all the time, when I never deserve it. I want to be merciful, too, but often I care more about fairness than mercy. Help me to be quick to forgive or overlook an offense. Help me to have compassion for those in need. In Jesus' name, Amen.

The heart with helping hands reminds you to reach out in love to others who need your help.

Gratitude

is being thankful to God and others for the good things I have been given.

"Give thanks in all circumstances,

for this is

God's will

for you in

Christ

Jesus."

—1 Thessalonians 5:18

Gratitude is being thankful to God and others for the good things I have been given.

EXAMPLES:

1. I should thank my mom for providing dinner, even when it's not something I really like.

2. I should be grateful that my parents teach me to obey.

....

....

....

....

....

....

PRAYER: O Lord, I ask that you would give me a grateful heart. Too often I accept your blessings as though I deserve them, and complain about what I don't have. You have given the greatest gift of all—Jesus Christ. Please help me to be truly grateful. In Jesus' name, Amen.

The smiling flowers receive life-giving rain. In the same way, be grateful that God gives you everything you need.

Respect

is showing appropriate honor and obedience to God, to the authorities he has placed over me, and to my neighbor.

"Show proper **respect** to everyone: Love the brotherhood of believers, fear God, honor the king."
—1 Peter 2:17

Respect is showing appropriate honor and obedience to God, to all the authorities he has placed over me, and to my neighbor.

1. I should show respect by not interrupting others.

2. I must always pay attention and be polite to my

parents and teachers.

PRAYER: Lord, help me to respect others, especially those in authority over me. Even when I think someone is wrong or unfair, help me to be sincerely respectful out of love and respect for you. In Jesus' name, Amen.

The wooden toy soldier's salute shows proper respect for authority.

Trust

is believing and doing what God tells me in the Bible, even when it is hard to do.

"**Trust** in the Lord with all your heart and lean not on your own understanding. In **all** your ways acknowledge him, and he will make your paths straight."
—Proverbs 3:5,6

Trust is believing and doing what God tells me in the Bible, even when it is hard to do.

EXAMPLES:

1. I will trust God when my parents go away on vacation and I miss them.

2. I should trust God and go to sleep when I'm afraid of the dark.

PRAYER: Father in heaven, please help me to trust you. Thank you that you are in control of everything and you do everything for my good. You have promised to take care of me. Help me to believe and act on that, even when I'm afraid. In Jesus' name, Amen.

The boy holds his father's hand and follows him wherever he leads. You should trust God in the same way.

Truthfulness

is telling information accurately, without exaggerating or misleading.

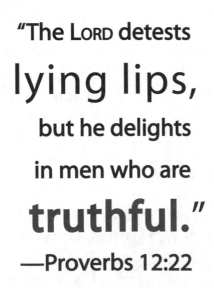

"The LORD detests **lying lips,** but he delights in men who are **truthful."**

—Proverbs 12:22

Truthfulness is telling information accurately, without exaggerating or misleading.

EXAMPLES:

1. When I haven't done my homework, I shouldn't

tell my teacher that I did it but then the dog ate it.

2. I shouldn't blame my sister for a fight when I started it.

_____

_____

_____

_____

_____

_____

PRAYER: Lord, help me to be truthful. Sometimes I'm afraid if I tell the truth I'll get in trouble or someone will be angry at me. Thank you that Jesus died to pay for all the sins of his people. Please give me the courage to please you by being truthful. In Jesus' name, Amen.

The arrow hit the target dead center. Your words should hit the target of truth, too — dead center.

Patience

is accepting problems without complaining, trusting that God will care for me.

"And we know that in **all things** God works for the good of those who love him, who have been called according to his purpose."

—Romans 8:28

Patience is accepting problems without complaining, trusting that God will care for me.

EXAMPLES:

1. I should be patient when I'm starving and dinner isn't ready yet.

2. When daddy is going to take me out for dinner, but he's late getting home from work, I can be patient.

....

....

....

....

....

....

PRAYER: Dear God, you are always patient and loving with me. Please help me to be patient, too. I know that you cause everything to happen for my good, and you work things out at the right time. Help me to trust you and not complain when things are difficult. In Jesus' name, Amen.

The dog waits patiently for his master to feed him. So should you wait for God without complaining, trusting that he will care for you.

Meekness

is being willing to give up my rights in order to put others first. Meekness waits for God to bring about justice.

"A little while, and the **wicked** will be no more; Though you look for them, they will not be found. But the meek will inherit the land and enjoy great peace."
—Psalm 37:10-11

Meekness is being willing to give up my rights in order to put others first. Meekness waits for God to bring about justice.

EXAMPLES:

1. When my little brother forgets to pick up his toys, I can remind him nicely and help him instead of telling on him.

2. When my classmate is failing math and wants to copy my homework, I should not let him, but I can offer to help him study instead of looking down on him.

PRAYER: Lord, help me to remember my own sinfulness, and help me to love others without thinking I'm better than they are. Help me to care more about what you want than about myself. In Jesus' name, Amen.

The bear, who could be fierce and dangerous, chooses to be gentle and bring flowers. So you should be peaceful and leave vengeance to God.

Discernment

is seeing the difference between good and bad—or good and best—so I know what to do to please God.

"Above all else, guard your **heart,** for it is the wellspring of life ...

Make **level paths** for your feet and take only **ways** that are **firm.**

—Proverbs 4:23, 26

Discernment is seeing the difference between good and bad — or good and best — so I know what to do to please God.

EXAMPLES:

1. I shouldn't imitate movie stars or singers if they behave in ways that are disobedient to God, even if I like some things about them.

2. I can pay attention when I am taught about the Bible, so I can learn what God wants and recognize when things are wrong.

PRAYER: Dear Lord, sin makes me so foolish and stupid sometimes! Thank you for giving us the Bible for wisdom. Help me to think carefully about what is best and do it, even if that means disagreeing with my friends. Please help me to love wisdom and be discerning. In Jesus' name, Amen.

The signpost shows several ways to go; the children must choose the best way. You, too, must learn to make the best choices.

Faithfulness

is being dependable, so that others can trust what I say and do.

"Let love and
faithfulness
never leave you.
Bind them around your neck,
Write them on the tablet of your heart."
—Proverbs 3:3

Faithfulness is being dependable, so that others can trust what I say and do.

EXAMPLES:

1. If I promised to play with my sister after school, I should not change my mind when my best friend invites me over.

2. I should do my work—and do it well—even when no one is checking on me.

PRAYER: Dear God, it's hard to be faithful all the time. I just can't do it. Even when I'm trying, I fail a lot. Please help me to be more and more trustworthy and dependable. Thank you that Jesus was completely faithful for me. In Jesus' name, Amen.

The rainbow is the sign of God's covenant with all living creatures that promises he will never again destroy all life with a flood (Gen. 9:12). Just as God is always faithful to his Word, so you should be faithful in all you say and do.

Joyfulness

is believing that God will work all things together for my good, so I never have to despair. I can be joyful even when I am sad.

"Shout for **joy** to the LORD, all the earth."
—Psalm 100:1

Joyfulness is believing that God will work things together for my good, so I never have to despair. I can be joyful even when I am sad.

EXAMPLES:

1. I can be joyful even when I am disappointed that I had to cancel my birthday party because I'm sick.

2. I can be joyful even when my dog dies and I'm very sad.

PRAYER: O Father, thank you that Jesus died to take away sin and sadness and that you always care for me. Help me to be joyful, even in times when I am sad. Thank you that everything you do is good and right. In Jesus' name, Amen.

Joy shows in the boy's face, even though he is calm. In the same way, you should always have joy in the Lord, even when life is difficult.

Self-control

is the ability to say no to my wrong desires and yes to what God wants me to do.

"Like a city whose walls are broken down is a man who lacks self-control."

—Proverbs 25:28

Self-control is the ability to say no to my wrong desires and yes to what God wants me to do.

EXAMPLES:

1. I should control myself to be meek and patient when others laugh at me because I won't use bad language or look at bad pictures.

2. I should say no to myself when I want to take some cookies I'm not supposed to eat.

PRAYER: Father, please help me to say no to sin and yes to obedience and pleasing you. I really want to do whatever you want me to do, but it's too hard by myself. I need your help all the time to say "yes" to you. Please help me. In Jesus' name, Amen.

The gymnast must have control of every muscle to perform on the balance beam. You must learn spiritual self-control to obey God.

Diligence

is working without getting distracted or stopping before I'm supposed to.

"Go to the ant, you sluggard; consider its ways and be wise!"

—Proverbs 6:6

Diligence is working without getting distracted or stopping before I'm supposed to.

1. I should do my homework without stopping to play.

2. I should do all my chores before I play.

....

....

....

....

....

....

....

PRAYER: Lord, thank you that Jesus was always diligent and finished his work of saving sinners. It's so easy for me to forget to finish my work. Sometimes I just don't feel like doing what I'm supposed to do, and I do other things instead. Please help me to be diligent and faithful like Jesus was. In Jesus' name, Amen.

Ants keep on working. You should follow their example of diligence.

Repentance

is changing my mind and turning around to do the right thing.

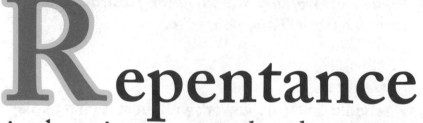

"He who **conceals** his sins does not prosper, but whoever **confesses** and **renounces** them finds **mercy.**"

—Proverbs 28:13

Repentance is changing my mind and turning around to do the right thing.

EXAMPLES:

1. When I have been lazy, I should repent and start doing my work, instead of making excuses.

2. When I'm sad and cry because I don't like my dinner, I should repent and finish eating with a pleasant attitude.

....

....

....

....

....

PRAYER: God, thank you for making repentance possible by sending Jesus to live and die in my place. Thank you that my sin doesn't separate me from your love. But still, sometimes it's hard to repent, especially when I am stubborn and angry and I just want my own way. Please give me a repentant heart and help me to love you more. In Jesus' name, Amen.

Just as the arrow shows a complete turnaround, so you should repent and turn away from sin.

Kindness

is being thoughtful and quick to do good to others.

"...Love is **kind**...."

—1 Corinthians 13:4

Kindness is being thoughtful and quick to do good to others.

EXAMPLES:

1. I should run to help anyone who gets hurt.

2. I should notice when other kids are being left out and try to talk to them and include them.

_____

_____

_____

_____

_____

_____

_____

PRAYER: Father, thank you for your kindness to me. Thank you for forgiving my sin. Please help me to be kind, too, and think more about others. Help me to notice when people need something, and help me be quick to do good for them, even when it's not convenient for me. In Jesus' name, Amen.

One boy is taking care of the other boy. In the same way, you should always be kind to others.

Justice

is measuring everything by God's law, to know and do what is right.

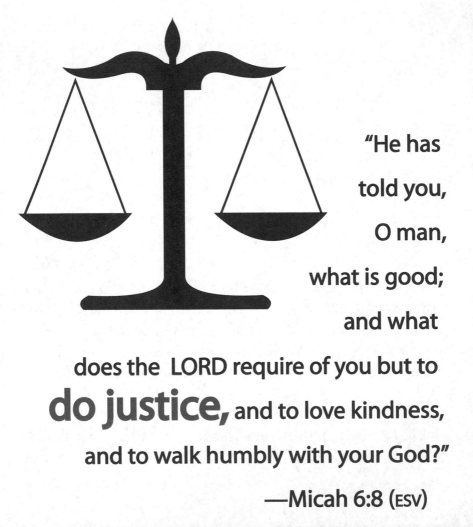

"He has told you, O man, what is good; and what does the LORD require of you but to **do justice,** and to love kindness, and to walk humbly with your God?"

—Micah 6:8 (ESV)

Justice is measuring everything by God's law, to know and do what is right.

EXAMPLES:

1. I should obey even when no one is looking, because I want to please God.

2. I shouldn't listen to gossip about others and assume it is true; instead, I should think the best.

PRAYER: Father, you are perfectly right in everything you do. Thank you that Jesus was perfectly right and just for me. Help me to act with justice and to walk faithfully in your ways. Help me to love your law and your righteousness. In Jesus' name, Amen.

The balance scale measures what is in one pan against the weight in the other pan. So, too, we should measure our thoughts, words, and actions by how close they come to God's perfect law.

Gentleness

is using only the strength or force that is appropriate.

"The fruit of the Spirit is...

gentleness."

Galatians 5:22-23

Gentleness is using only the strength or force that is appropriate.

1. I should be gentle with my baby brother when

he is fussy.

2. When I have to correct my friends, I should be gentle

and meek.

PRAYER: Lord, thank you for being kind and gentle with me, even when I'm not acting right. I know sometimes I'm too loud and rough. I don't mean to hurt or offend people, but sometimes I do. Please help me to be gentle. In Jesus' name, Amen.

The girl waits quietly and gently for the goat to eat from her hand, not startling it or scaring it away. You should be gentle too, remembering how easy it is to frighten or hurt others without meaning to.

Humility

is knowing that everything good in me is from God alone, and is not for my benefit first, but for serving God and others. I shouldn't put myself first.

"In **humility** consider others better than yourselves.

—Philippians 2:3

Humility is knowing that everything good in me is from God alone, and is not for my benefit first, but for serving God and others. I shouldn't put myself first.

EXAMPLES:

1. I shouldn't brag about myself and things I can do.

2. I should let others go first when we're taking turns.

PRAYER: Father, thank you for Jesus, who humbled himself for sinners like me, when he didn't have to. Please help me to put others first like Jesus did; so often I put myself first. Help me to be humble instead of proud and to think of others and try to serve them first. In Jesus' name, Amen.

Jesus humbled himself by becoming a man, born as a baby. Apart from God's gifts, you are as helpless as a newborn baby. You have nothing to be proud of except God.

Courage

is doing what must be done, even when I am afraid and I think it is too hard.

Be strong and

courageous.

Do not be

terrified;

do not be

discouraged,

for the LORD your God will be

with you wherever you go."

—Joshua 1:9

Courage is doing what must be done, even when I am afraid and I think it is too hard.

EXAMPLES:

1. I can go to a new school where I don't know anybody, even if I am scared .

2. When my friends wear clothes that aren't modest, I can have the courage to be different so I can please God.

PRAYER: God, please help me to have courage. It's very hard to to do what's right when people might make fun of me or be angry at me. It's also hard when I'm afraid I'll fail. Thank you for Jesus, who had the courage to die on the cross for me. Help me to care about pleasing you more than anything else. In Jesus' name, Amen.

The ant has an impossible task, but he is attacking the huge stone with great courage and valor. You should have courage to do anything God wants you to do, because he will be with you, and all things are possible with God.

Love

is giving willingly of whatever
I have to meet someone's need.

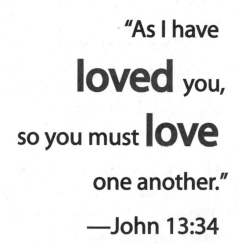

"As I have **loved** you,
so you must **love**
one another."
—John 13:34

Love is giving willingly of whatever I have to meet someone's need.

EXAMPLES:

1. I can love my big brother by helping him rake leaves so he can finish his work before his game starts.

2. When my dad and mom are tired, I can love them by playing a game with my little sister so they can rest.

PRAYER: Lord, you love me perfectly. I want to be like Jesus, but often I'm selfish before I even think about it. I need your grace every day to help me to love others. Thank you for helping me to grow and be more like Jesus. In Jesus' name, Amen.

Jesus loved us and sacrificed himself for us on the cross. So, too, you should sacrifice whatever is needed in order to show love to God and others.

Lesson 1: Listening

Opening activity: Each child is assigned 1 of 3 animal sounds. All the children simultaneously moo, bark, meow, etc., while finding all the other "animals" like him. First group to find everyone wins.

Point of game: You have to practice listening carefully to become skilled at paying attention and learning from others.

Memory verse: Proverbs 4:1 "Listen, my sons, to a father's instruction; pay attention and gain understanding."

Definition: Listening is giving careful attention to another person. Listening is a way to show a person love and respect.

Discussion:

- What do you think when someone doesn't listen to you?

- When someone speaks to you, do you stop what you're doing, look at him, and listen?

- Is it more fun to be the "talker" or the "listener"?

- If you do ALL the talking, whom are you considering as best?

- Listening shows love and respect by saying, "What you are saying is important to me."

"In humility consider others better than yourselves."
— Philippians 2:3

Lesson 2: Obedience

Opening activity: Red Light, Green Light — The children line up facing the leader. When the leader says, "Red Light" the children must not move; when the leader says, "Green Light" the children may advance; anyone who moves during a "red light" has to return to the beginning. The first one to reach the leader wins.

Memory verse: Colossians 3:20 "Children, obey your parents in everything, for this pleases the Lord."

Definition: Obedience is doing exactly what I am asked to do, right away, with a willing attitude.

Discussion:

- Whom do you have to obey? *Your parents.*

- How do you know you have to obey your parents? *God says so in the Bible.*

- Why do you have to obey God? *Because he made you. Since he made you, he has the right to tell you what to do. He also has control of everything, and you can't get away from his consequences (or his punishments).*

- Is it fun to obey? *Sometimes it's really hard!!!!*

- Why is it so hard to obey? *Because we want to do what WE want to do.*

- Are you happy after you obey? *Yes, if you really obey with a good attitude, because God's way is always BEST, even when it's very hard.*

- How can you have a willing attitude when you have to do something you don't want to do? *You can want to please God more than you want your own way. So you can do something you really, really don't want to do ... but you do it anyway, because you want to please God and obey him.*

Role play games: (Kids can act out "obedience" that isn't really obedience because it's doing what they're told, but not exactly, with delay, or grudgingly). Have the other students tell what's wrong with their "obedience":

- Mom says, "It's time for bed; put your book (or toys, or games) away and get your pajamas on!

- Teacher says, "Class, no talking. Please pay attention."

- Dad says, "Stop talking and finish your dinner!"

- Mom says, "Go do your homework before you do anything else."

- Dad says, "Please take out the garbage before you play."

What if I just don't want to obey—it's TOO hard?
Pray and ask God to forgive you and help you,
and change your heart to love him and obey him.

"Although He was a Son,
He learned obedience from what He suffered."
—Hebrews 5:8

Lesson 3: Contentment

Opening activity: Have a page or two of pictures of things that children might like or dislike. Let the children draw happy or sad faces on the pictures to indicate what they like or don't like.

Memory verse: Philippians 4:11 "I have learned to be content whatever the circumstances."

Definition: Contentment is trusting that God is in control of everything, and he is working everything in my life together for my good and for his glory.

Discussion:

Is it hard to be content when

- You get sick on the day of your own birthday party? *Yes.*
- You get the most Christmas presents ever? *No.*
- Your mom makes chocolate chip cookies and you can have as many as you want? *No.*
- You get disciplined? *Yes.*
- You get brand new shoes? *No.*
- You have to clean your room before you can play? *Yes.*

What things are you discontent about?

- Wanting to do things you're not allowed to do?
- Wanting to be older?
- Being bored with …
- Being treated unfairly? Such as?
- What "good" thoughts can you think to help you be content?

- If you are disappointed and angry about something, but you act polite and pleasant, are you truly content? *No.*

- If your sister is unkind to your brother, and you're angry about it, should you be content? How should you respond? *Lovingly confront her (Gal. 6:1, If you catch a brother in a sin, go to him ....) and remind her how God wants her to act; if she won't listen or change, tell her you both have to go talk to your mom and dad.*

When it's too hard to be content, pray & ask God to help you trust that he is doing what's best; talk to parents, a Christian teacher, or your pastor for advice and help.

Role play games: Have groups of 2 or 3 act out how to be content when it's difficult:

- Your mom tells you "no" when you ask to have a friend stay overnight.

- Your friend accidentally breaks your favorite toy.

- You go to someone's house for dinner and they serve liver and spinach (which you don't like).

- Your friends are all going to the beach, but you can't go.

- Your dad was going to take you to a movie, but he had to work instead.

Remember that God brings hard things to help you grow; and remember that Jesus was content to suffer for you.

"Therefore I am well content with weaknesses, with insults, with distresses, with persecutions, with difficulties, for Christ's sake; for when I am weak, then I am strong." —2 Corinthians 12:10 (NASV)

Lesson 4: Orderliness

Opening activity: Verse scramble: Print out a verse or a sentence in large letters. Cut the sentence into individual words or phrases. Give each child one piece of paper. Children should line themselves up so that the words are in proper order.

Definition: Orderliness is keeping things in the right place and doing things at the right time.

Memory verse: 1 Corinthians 14:33 "God is not a God of disorder but of peace."

Discussion: Some kinds of orderliness are to help you be considerate, e.g. "indoor" behavior

God's order: work first, then rest or play.

- *E.g. ants work in summer (Prov 6:6–8) "Go to the ant , O sluggard, Observe her ways and be wise, Which, having no chief, officer or ruler, prepares her food in the summer and gathers her provision in the harvest."*

What can we do to promote orderliness? (List)

- *Keep room clean, help fold laundry, do housework*
- *Go to bed on time and get up on time*
- *Get ready for church, school, etc., on time*

Role play games: Sequencing of tasks (In random order, list all the steps involved in each task, then have the children put them in proper sequence.)

Homework   Cleaning room   Making cookies

You see, at **just the right time**, when we were still powerless, Christ died for the ungodly. —Romans 5:6

Lesson 5: Mercy

Opening activity: Review briefly the definitions of obedience, listening, truthfulness, respect. Teacher and/or students act out each behavior for children to identify:

NOT listening	Truthfulness
Listening	Deceit
Obedience	Respect
DISobedience	DISrespect

Memory verse: Ephesians 4:32 "Be kind and compassionate to one another, forgiving each other, just as in Christ God forgave you."

Definition: Mercy is showing kindness to those who are weak, sinful, and needy, because Christ loved me first when I was his enemy (like the parable of the good Samaritan).

Discussion: How can you be merciful? Think of specific opportunities.

- Who is weak? *Anyone younger or smaller than you are (esp. siblings); anyone under your authority.*

- *Who is sinful and needy? Everyone, sometimes. Anyone who is hurt, sick, poor, unhappy, troubled, etc.*

- *Are needy people attractive and fun? Not usually. But how do you want to be treated when you're miserable?*

Role Play Games: Have the children role play ways to show mercy in the situations discussed above.

"We love because He first loved us." —1 John 4:19

Lesson 6: Gratitude

Opening activity: Review by cutting apart words, definitions, pictures & verses of each quality. Have kids match them up.

Definition: Gratitude is being thankful to God and others for the good things I have been given.

Memory verse: I Thessalonians 5:18 "Give thanks in all circumstances, for this is God's will for you in Christ Jesus."

Discussion:
*   What do we sometimes do instead of expressing gratitude? *Forget to say thank you, complain, whine.*

*   When we aren't grateful, what are we doing instead? *Thinking of ourselves and what we want.*

*   What should we do to be grateful? *Remember that we deserve nothing but punishment from God!*

Role play games: Leader says something to a student, such as giving a compliment, describing a gift or activity. The student thinks of an appropriate way to express gratitude.

*   Do your homework now. Start with your math, please.

*   We're going to the zoo tomorrow.

*   Dinner's ready! Steak with brussel sprouts!

*   Would you like me to help you clean your room?

*   Here is your snack. I know it's not what you asked for, but it's what we have today.

How great is the love the Father has lavished on us,
that we should be called children of God! —1 John 3:1a

Lesson 7: Respect

Opening activity: Introduce new character quality. Show picture of toy soldier saluting. Discuss saluting as a way of showing respect for rank.

Definition: Respect is showing appropriate honor and obedience to God, to the authorities he has placed over me, and to my neighbor.

Memory verse: 1 Peter 2:17 "Show proper respect to everyone: Love the brotherhood of believers, fear God, honor the king." (ESV)

Discussion: How should we show respect for God, authorities, and neighbors? Some simple ways are:

- Knock before entering someone's room.
- Address people appropriately, using proper titles, or "sir" and "ma'am." Say "please" and "thank you."
- Do not interrupt or contradict others unnecessarily; when necessary, do so in a kind and tactful way.
- Speak pleasantly, and speak well of others.
- Follow rules & obey laws.

Role play games: Each child picks a paper and plays the role of the person named. In each group, one person is the authority; the others must find ways to show respect.

Policeman:	*Officer Donnelly*	*Officer*
President:	*President Bush*	*Mr. President*
Governor:	*Governor Smith*	*Governor Smith*
Judge:	*Judge Mitchell*	*Your Honor*

" ... but in your hearts honor Christ the Lord as holy .... "
—1 Peter 3:15a

Lesson 8: Trust

Opening activity: Blindfold Walk—Divide group into pairs. One wears a blindfold, the other leads him around the room twice. The first time, the guide describes the route; the second time, the guide is silent.

Definition: Trust is believing what God says in the Bible and living as though I believe him, even when it's hard.

Memory verse: Proverbs 3:5, 6 "Trust in the Lord with all your heart and lean not on your own understanding; in all your ways acknowledge him, and he will make your paths straight."

Discussion: Relate the definition of trust to the story of Eve's temptation by the serpent. Review the story in Genesis 3.

Did Eve trust God's Word with all her heart, or did she listen to Satan's word? Did she lean on her own understanding?

How should Eve have answered Satan? (Ask the children to suggest answers she could have given.) For example,

- *Let's go find Adam. I want him to hear you, too!*

- *No, he said we could eat from all the trees except the tree of knowledge of good and evil. If we eat fruit from that tree we will die.*

- *I believe God. If he said we would die if we eat that fruit, then we will. I won't even think about eating it.*

- *I trust God. If he doesn't want us to know evil, then I don't want to know evil.*

Role play games: Ask the children—

When is it hard to trust God? Your parents? *When you are afraid? When you want something else more than you want to please God?*

What are you afraid of? *The dark; separation from parents; punishment; thunderstorms; snakes or spiders; people not liking you; people thinking you're stupid or you're a dork.*

Have the children do role plays using these Bible verses (or others) to help them trust God in scary situtations, instead of disobeying or being afraid.

- *Psalm 56:4 "In God, whose word I praise, in God I trust; I will not be afraid. What can mortal man do to me?"*

- *Psalm 121:7-8 "The LORD will keep you from all harm— he will watch over your life; the LORD will watch over your coming and going both now and forevermore."*

- *John 10:27-28 "My sheep listen to my voice; I know them, and they follow me. I give them eternal life, and they shall never perish; no one can snatch them out of my hand."*

- *Proverbs 3:5-6 "Trust in the Lord with all your heart and lean not on your own understanding; in all your ways acknowledge him, and he will make your paths straight."*

I will say of the LORD,
"He is my refuge and my fortress,
my God, in whom I trust." —Psalm 91:2

Lesson 9: Truthfulness

Opening activity: True-or-False Game   Make a series of statements. Children answer "true" or "false." For example:

- Cows are green.
- Parents are perfect.
- The Bible is all true.
- Grass is red.
- Ice cream is delicious.

- The sky is blue.
- God can't see in the dark.
- There is only one God.
- Whales live in the ocean.
- Monkeys live at the North Pole.

The point of the game: "Some things are true and some things are false. Is it important to know the difference? *Yes!*"

Memory verse: Proverbs 12:22 "The Lord detests lying lips, but he delights in men who are truthful."

Definition: Truthfulness is telling information accurately, without exaggerating or misleading.

Discussion:

Do you know what it means to exaggerate? Do you know what it means to mislead?

For example, a child could report an incident in 3 different ways:

- He HIT my leg, and I can't walk! I think it's broken!!!

- He's mean! He kicked me and knocked me down!

- I stuck my foot out to trip him, and he kicked me. I lost my balance and tripped him.

  - *Which one do you think is the truth? (c)*

- *Which one is exaggerating? (a)*
- *Which one is misleading? (b)*

Is it all right to tell made-up stories? Is it truthful?

- *Yes, as long as everyone knows it is just "pretend" and you're not misleading anyone. Otherwise, if you are trying to deceive or mislead, it becomes a lie.*

- *Made-up stories are called "fiction." Jesus used a form of fiction when he told parables to teach his followers.*

Why is it hard to be truthful sometimes?

- *When we've done something wrong, and we don't want others to know. We don't want to get in trouble.*

- *We are afraid that others will look down on us or laugh at us if they know the truth. We want people to think well of us.*

- *Sometimes we are tempted to lie so we can get something we want—and we want that thing more than we want to please God.*

Jesus answered, "I am the way and the truth and the life.
No one comes to the Father except through me.
—John 14:6

Lesson 10: Patience

Opening activity: What is the dog doing? *(Waiting patiently for his dinner.)* Talk about how hard it is to be patient when we're hungry and waiting for food.

Memory verse: Romans 8:28 "And we know that in all things God works for the good of those who love him, who have been called according to his purpose."

Definition: Patience is accepting all the problems God gives me with a willing and quiet attitude, trusting that he will care for me.

Discussion: When is it hard to be patient?

- On Christmas morning?

- When your parents are talking and you're waiting to play?

- When your little sister or brother wants to play with you and your friend, but they slow you down?

- When you're not allowed to watch a show that your friends may watch?

How should you think about the problem in order to work at being patient?

- Who is in control? *God*

- Does God do good or bad things for me? *Good things.*

- Why does God make hard things happen to us? *To train us, for our good.*

- Is that good or bad? *Good*

- Should you complain? *No*

- When it seems too hard, what should you do? *Pray and ask God to help you be patient.*

Role play games:

- The person in front of you in line just took the last piece of the dessert you wanted.

- You are watching your favorite TV show, and your sister keeps interrupting you, asking you to help her with her homework.

- You're trying to finish your chores so you can play, and your mom and dad keep adding extra tasks to do.

- At dinnertime, you're trying to tell your family about something exciting that you did, but you keep getting interrupted.

The Lord is not slow in keeping his promise,
as some understand slowness.
He is patient with you, not wanting anyone to
perish, but everyone to come to repentance.
—2 Peter 3:9

Lesson 11: Meekness

Opening activity: Review. Print out the definitions, pictures & verses of each quality; cut apart the words. Have kids match them up.

Definition: Meekness is being willing to give up my rights in order to put God and others first. Meekness waits for God to bring about justice.

Memory verse: Psalm 37:10, 11
"A little while, and the wicked will be no more;
   Though you look for them, they will not be found.
But the meek will inherit the land
   And enjoy great peace."

Discussion: What do we "need," and what do we "want"?

Need:	*Want:*
Food	Fast food, candy
Clothes	Fun friends
Shelter	Toys
Parents	Video games

Now let's talk about rights. What do we have a "right" to? Only what God says we have a right to. And what is that?

- Food? *(he will provide)*
- Clothes? *(he will provide)*
- Parents? *(he is our father)*
- Shelter? *(he is our rock, fortress, hiding place. Jesus didn't have his own home)*
- Toys? *(no)*
- Fun friends? *(no. Jesus loved the unlovely—the bad people, the poor and unpopular people. He said to love your neighbor as yourself. Do you want kids to play with you only if you're the most popular?)*

If everyone would love others, you would always be treated well. But that doesn't happen, does it? Sometimes people aren't nice—or fun—or even fair. Jesus wants you to stop thinking about what you want and what's fair, and put others first. Trust God to take care of what's fair—he'll work it out eventually; only he knows what's really best anyway.

Role Plays: The following scenarios provide opportunities for children to practice meekness. Assign each scenario to a group of two or three children:

- Your brother or your friend takes a longer turn at the video game than he should. How should you respond?

- You go without your dessert to let your little sister have a serving. There's not enough to go around because she spilled hers.

- Your older brother has friends over, so you decide not to ask to play with them.

- You include your younger brothers or sisters in some of your activities when you have your friends over.

- There's no money for new clothes at Easter. Someone gives your sister a great new outfit, but you have to wear a dress from last year.

Jesus knew that the time had come for him to leave this world and go to the Father. Having loved his own who were in the world, he now showed them the full extent of his love ... he poured water into a basin and began to wash his disciples' feet ...." —John 13:1b, 5

Lesson 12: Discernment

Opening activities:

Use optical illusions to discuss that you often have to think carefully about what you're seeing. It might look like one thing, but really be something else.

Make an obstacle course: scatter some chairs, toys, clothes, and books. Have several children walk through it. Make it challenging to get through. Then, make a "level path" and have them go through again, easily. Ask which path they would rather walk in the dark.

Then, introduce the memory verse, and talk about how we can guard our hearts by making level paths for our feet. When we think about what pleases God and choose to follow his ways over and over, we make level paths. We recognize the right ways more quckly. Obedience becomes a familiar, level path, and we don't make better decisions.

Memory verse: Proverbs 4: 23, 26
> Above all else, guard your heart,
>> for it is the wellspring of life…
> Make level paths for your feet
>> and take only ways that are firm.

Definition: Discernment is seeing the difference between good and bad—or good and best—so I know what to do to please God.

Discussion: As you get older, mom and dad aren't always there to tell you what to do. You yourself have to decide what is right. That's discernment. Here are some examples:

- Mom says to do homework before playing. You start your homework; Your baby brother, Ryan, starts fussing, and your brother plays with Ryan to keep him happy.

Which is better? Doing homework or playing with Ryan? What is best?

- You have two new families on your street. Jennifer is very friendly and fun; she comes over to play almost every day after school. Ethan is quiet and doesn't come out much. You and your brother think Ethan probably doesn't like you. What should you do?

- All your friends are reading popular books. Or, all your friends are watching a popular new movie. Should you? How do you decide if something is good or bad?

You always have to ask, "Does this please and honor God?" How does it honor God? How does it not honor God?

Ask your parents, but realize that you also have to think about it yourself. The issue is not just whether you're allowed to watch or read something, it's also an issue for you to learn how to choose what's important to you.

- When you turn 16, you have a choice of two jobs: one is at a fast-food restaurant; one is at a popular shop where kids can get tattoos and body piercing. Is one job better than the other job? Why is it good to get a job?

Discuss their responsibility to think about pleasing God, especially as they spend more time away from parents. When situations arise for which rules haven't been made, loving God means they have to decide for themselves what pleases Him.

Role Play: Have the children role play the situations described in the opening activity.

Direct me in the path of your commands, for there I find delight.
—Psalm 119:35

Lesson 13: Faithfulness

Opening activity: Make a set of cards, each with one character trait on it. Give each child a card. Ask them to hold it up when you describe a situation that requires that trait to be practiced. (More than one trait will be required.) After describing several situations, introduce faithfulness.

Memory verse: Proverbs 3:3 "Let love and faithfulness never leave you; bind them around your neck, write them on the tablet of your heart."

Show an identification necklace or bracelet, and describe how some people wear an I.D. all the time (e.g., for a medical condition). In the same way, faithfulness is like something we wear all the time.

Definition: Faithfulness is being dependable, so that others can trust what you say and do.

Discussion: Discuss how faithfulness means obeying God all the time, even when no one but God is watching. When can you take a break from being faithful? *Never!*

Re-distribute the character trait cards. Ask the children to tell how "their" trait is required in the following situations:

- You are very, very tired. Your mom asks you to put away your little sister's toys before you go to bed. What character qualities do you NEED? *obedience, contentment, orderliness, gratitude, respect, trust, patience*

- You are sick and you feel terrible. You mom is taking care of you, but she has to take care of your baby brother, too, and the rest of the family. What character qualities do you NEED? *obedience, contentment, grati-*

tude, respect, trust, patience

- You wake up after a scary dream. Your mom and dad talk to you, but you're still upset. What character qualities do you need? *trust, contentment, respect, self-control*

- Your best friend just moved to another state and you're very sad. What character qualities do you need? *gratitude, contentment, trust, patience*

- Your little brother or sister ruined your favorite shirt with mom's lipstick. What character qualities do you need? *meekness, mercy, gratitude, contentment, trust, patience*

Role play games: Have the children role play the situations described in the discussion questions above.

~~~~~~

I can do everything through him who gives me strength.
—Philippians 4:13

~~~~~~

Lesson 14: Joyfulness

Opening activity: Divide the children into groups; assign 1 or 2 of the following activities to each group: Singing. Shouting. Dancing. Laughing. Clapping. Feasting.

Give the signal to begin the actions. After a minute or so, stop and talk about what these actions usually express: JOYFULNESS! Explain that God made us to be joyful, and he wants us to sing, shout, dance, laugh, clap, and feast— a lot!

Memory verse: Psalm 100:1 "Shout for joy to the Lord, all the earth."

Definition: Joyfulness is believing that God will work all things together for my good, so I never have to despair. I can be joyful even when I am sad.

Discussion: Why should we shout for joy?

Psalm 100 says, Know that the Lord, he is God! He made us, and we are his; his love lasts forever.

- What does God's love do for you that should make you joyful? Have the children list examples of God's love: *parents & family, home, food, friends, church, school, creation's beauty, animals, the Bible, Jesus Christ.*

- The Bible says, "Be joyful always; pray continually; give thanks in all circumstances, for this is God's will for you in Christ Jesus" (1 Thessalonians 5:16-18). But when sad or hard things happen, how can you be joyful?

  When hard things happen you have to remind yourself
  - *that God causes all things to work together for the good of those who love him.*
  - *he brings trials to test you and help you grow (like*

exercises in physical education makes you stronger).

- *God himself never leaves you alone. He is the God of all comfort, and he will help you if you trust him (2 Corinthians 1:3–4).*

- Our joyfulness should always be "to the Lord," never joyfulness about sinning! Can you think of Bible stories where people were joyful in a bad way, not "to the Lord"?

  - *Israelites when they worshiped the golden calf.*

  - *The Philistines were having a party when Samson pulled down the pillars and everyone died.*

  - *Babylon, at the feast when the handwriting appeared on the wall.*

Role play games: Have small groups of 2 or 3 children role play opportunities to practice joyfulness in hard circumstances. Here are some examples to get started. Be sure that the children understand that joyfulness does not exclude appropriate sadness.

- A grandparent who is a Christian dies.

- A tree falls on your house and crashes through the roof, damaging your own bedroom.

- Your dad loses his job and there's not enough money to pay for _____(favorite activity).

- You get sick and miss two weeks of school, and you're too sick to even want to play or watch TV!

We wait in hope for the LORD; he is our help and our shield.
In him our hearts rejoice, for we trust in his holy name.
—Psalm 33:20-21

Lesson 15: Self-control

Opening activity: Pretend the children are a herd of sheep. Make a ring of chairs for a fence, with several gaps for them to escape through. The teacher is the shepherd, trying to keep the herd together inside the fence. Let them escape through the gaps to demonstrate how hard it would be to control the herd with a broken down fence.

Memory verse: Proverbs 25:28 "Like a city whose walls are broken down is a man who lacks self-control."

Definition: Self-control is the ability to say no to my wrong desires and yes to what God wants me to do.

Show the picture of the girl on the balance beam. Tell how she must have control over ALL her muscles, and how she must practice for many hours and days to learn that kind of self-control. In the same way, we must practice every day to learn the self-control to say yes to God.

Discussion: How is self-control like a fence? What is a fence for? It's to keep things in, and it's to keep other things out. A fence can keep your dog on your property, or keep children from running out into the street. Or it can keep people or animals from coming onto your property. For example, you might fence a garden to keep animals from coming in and eating your vegetables.

Self-control stops you from doing wrong things you want to do. Self-control is like a fence that stops your wrong desires from taking you in the wrong direction, and learning self control is like practicing to be a gymnast.

Here are some examples. In these situations, what is the wrong desire that we must say "no" to? What does self-control say "yes" to? Can you think of more examples?

- No one is looking, and Mom left some candy on the kitchen table.
- Mom forgot to tell me to do my homework … maybe I could play a game first.
- Mom's gone and Dad's watching football. They'll never notice if I watch that show I'm not supposed to.
- She is so mean and unkind. I'm not supposed to lose my temper, but she makes me so mad I can't help it!
- I studied for this test so hard, and I can almost remember the answer. I can see the test of the person next to me, and if I just lean over a little bit I can read the answer. I'd know if it was right or wrong ....

Role Play: Divide the children into small groups. Assign each group one of the examples above. Have them role play the "inner dialog" that one person might carry on when trying to practice self-control, with each child offering an argument (one at a time) either for or against self-control. For example:

- *I'm hungry. One piece of candy can't hurt.*
- *I'll be sorry afterward if I disobey.*
- *Mom & Dad won't even notice. If they were here they'd let me have some.*
- *God can see me, and he wants me to obey.*
- *If I pray, he'll help me do the right thing.*
- *I'm going to the other room so I won't keep thinking about disobeying!*

~~~~~~

"The one who sent me is with me; he has not left me alone, for I always do what pleases him." —John 8:29

Every day we fail in many ways, but Jesus' obedience is ours if we are his.

~~~~~~

Lesson 16: Diligence

Opening activity: Watch ants, if possible. Try putting a tiny crumb where they can collect it and watch them carry it into the anthill. Or, just describe how ants keep busy doing their jobs and are impossible to distract. Then, have the children pretend to be ants; put some small obstacles in their way for them to overcome.

Memory verse: Proverbs 6:6 "Go to the ant, you sluggard; consider its ways and be wise!"

Definition: Diligence is working without getting distracted or stopping before I'm supposed to.

Discussion: Everybody gets distracted from their work sometimes.

- What kinds of things distract you? *Things you love to do? TV? Reading a book? Talking? Playing? Getting a snack? Drawing?*

- When is it easiest to get distracted? *When you're doing something you don't like to do anyway? Doing homework? Cleaning your room? Eating your dinner (especially if you don't like it)? Doing your chores? What else?*

- It is easier to work hard when you really want to please someone, like your mom or dad, or a teacher, or a friend. Think of a time when you worked really diligently and enjoyed it. What made you want to do it? Were you thinking about someone who would be pleased or helped by what you did?

- Now, think about pleasing God, who loves you so-ooo much. Even when no one else is paying attention to you, you can please God by being diligent!

What are some ways you want to be more diligent?

Role Play: Have the children practice being diligent when they are tempted to:

- start playing while they are supposed to be cleaning their room.

- give up on their homework when it's taking too long or seems to hard.

- take a break to watch TV or read a book when they have chores they should finish first.

- avoid eating a meal they don't like .

Therefore,
since we are surrounded by so great a cloud of witnesses,
let us also lay aside every weight, and sin which clings so closely,
and **let us run with endurance** the race that is set before us,
looking to Jesus, the founder and perfecter of our faith,
who for the joy that was set before him endured the cross,
despising the shame, and is seated at the right hand
of the throne of God.   —Hebrews 12:1-2 (ESV)

Lesson 17: Repentance

Opening activity: Line the children up in several ranks and have them march, following your orders: Forward, march! Halt! Right-face, march! Left-face, march! About-face, march! Etc.

Then, show them the picture of the arrow and tell them that repentance is like doing an "about-face, march!"

Memory verse: Proverbs 28:13 "He who conceals his sins does not prosper, but whoever confesses and renounces them finds mercy."

When we sin, we're often tempted to hide the sin or pretend that it was just a mistake, and we didn't mean it. We don't want anyone else to know what we did. This verse tells us that we should repent of our sin.

Definition: Repentance is changing my mind and turning around to do the right thing.

Discussion:

- What should you do instead of concealing sin? Confess it and renounce it! Confessing and renouncing sin is the same thing as turning around and going in the opposite direction. When you renounce sin you stop doing it and leave it behind. You do the right thing, not the sin.

- Why do you think it is so hard to confess and renounce sin? It's embarrassing; we like the sin; we're afraid it will be too hard to stop; we're too scared of getting in trouble, we just don't want to admit we're wrong, etc.

- Let's think of some ways you could "hide your sin."

  Do the sin where your parents or family can't see; do it privately, when no one can see; have a bad attitude, but be nice and pleasant on the outside so no one knows what you're thinking.

- Why is it silly to try to hide your sin?

  Because God always sees you, and he will not let you get away with the sin, even if you don't get caught right away.

  Because the sin is hurting you and preventing you from prospering.

Role play: Have small groups of 2 or 3 children role-play repentance. Here are some examples to get started.

- Jared stole a candy bar at the store and hid it. His mom saw the empty wrapper later and asked him where it came from. He said someone gave it to him, but his lie bothered him, and he finally confessed to his parents. His dad took him to the store to confess and pay for the candy bar.

- Angela gossiped to her friends about a new girl in school and made fun of her clothes and and the way she talked. Another girl reminded her that she was being unkind and unmerciful with her words. At first Angela was angry at being rebuked, but then she felt sorry for the way she had talked. The next day she went to her friends and asked them to forgive her for her unkind gossip. Then she sat with the new girl at lunch and worked at being friendly.

- Zack cheated on his history test and his conscience bothered him. He went to his teacher later and confessed his sin. His teacher forgave him, but he gave him a zero for the test. Zack was sorry about the grade, but happy that the sin was taken care of.

But if Christ is in you, your body is dead because of sin, yet your spirit is alive because of righteousness. —Romans 8:10

Lesson 18: Kindness

Opening activity: Ask 2 or 3 children to act out some situations in which kindness is needed. The others have to guess what happened. For example:

- *A new student can't find the right classroom and is too shy to ask. She wanders around searching for the room .*

- *A child loses a shoe and can't find it.*

- *An old lady is trying to get her coat on, carry her handbag & book, and go out to the car—but she just started using a cane and she's having a hard time managing.*

Memory verse: 1 Corinthians 13:4 "Love is kind."

Definition: Kindness is being thoughtful and quick to do good to others.

Discussion: It's important to pay attention to other people and see when they need help. Usually we're busy doing things—playing, or talking, or eating—and we don't stop to think about the problems other people are having. But God wants you to be KIND, and that means you have to think about other people.

Notice others who are sad or upset, and never ignore them! If you're busy with your friends, what should you do? *Stop what you're doing and try to help!*

Role play: Have small groups of children role-play acts of kindness. Here are some examples to get started.

- You're all playing a game when your little sister falls down and hurts her knee. You're just about to win the game, but if you stop to help her, you probably won't win.

- A new student is in your class at church, but she doesn't seem very easy to talk to. You know you should be friendly, but you're shy, too.

  How should you think about this situation?
  An unfriendly person might just be shy, or maybe he is missing his friends at his old church; maybe he really does have a bad attitude and you will be able to help if you get to know him.

  What could you do? *Ask questions about his school, his family, what he likes to do—but don't pry; you can be pleasant even if he's not. Isn't that what you would want?*

- You come home from a big food shopping trip with your mom. Your favorite show is just starting. How can you be kind to your mom? *Help your mom bring in the groceries and put them away.*

- Another student is really having a hard time with schoolwork, but they don't say much because they're embarrassed and feel stupid. How can you be kind? *Never make fun of people. You can be sympathetic and share that some things are hard for you, too. If you're able, you could offer to help him study.*

But when the kindness and love of God our Savior appeared, he saved us, not because of righteous things we had done, but because of his mercy. —Titus 3:4-5a

Lesson 19: Justice

Opening activity: Show the children how a ruler can measure length, and also how you can see if something is uneven (Hold it against a piece of paper that is cut crookedly).

Show the picture of the balance scale, and explain how it works. *If you put a five lbs. weight in one pan, it will take five lbs. in the other pan to balance it.*

Memory verse: Micah 6:8 (ESV) "…what does the LORD require of you but to do justice, and to love kindness, and to walk humbly with your God."

Ask, "What does it mean, 'to do justice'?" Acknowledge that the phrase is a bit confusing, but that you'll explain it soon. Clearly, though, justice is important to God.

Definition: Justice is measuring everything by God's law, in order to know and do what is right.

Explain that God's law is like the balance weight, and like the straight edge of a ruler. Everything we do is measured by how it compares to God's law. We "do justice" by doing the things that God says are good and right.

Discussion: It's hard to do what is right. What do you do when you know what you should do, but you really want to do something else?

God wants you to love him so much that you'll try to do the right thing even when it's hard—he wants you to love doing justice. Justice means doing what his law says to do. God doesn't want you to obey just because you have to or you'll be in trouble. He wants you to love his way because it's so good! God's way is always the best, most happy way, even when it doesn't seem to be at first.

Here are some important questions about justice. You really, really need to know the answers to these questions!

- Does the balance scale of God's law show your actions to be too light? Or, when you measure your actions by the ruler of God's law, do your deeds line up straight against God's law? *No, we never measure up to God's law.*

- Then how can we ever please God? *Jesus always measured up and did everything perfectly. If God has forgiven our sins, he measures Jesus' deeds instead of ours.*

- Plus, when we belong to Jesus, the Holy Spirit helps us to change so we can learn to obey God more—even though we will always be sinful in this life. We are saved from our sin only by Jesus' perfectly obedient life and Jesus' death for us on the cross. But we do please God when we love and obey him.

Role play some examples of doing justice.
- One day you try to clean your room faster by shoving stuff under the bed—but you know that's wrong. *Doing justice means you go back and put everything where you're supposed to, even though no one else knows what you did.*

- When you do your math homework, you "accidentally" skip some problems (the ones that are hard) so you can be finished. *Doing justice means you go do them properly.*

- You found $20 in the laundry. Your Mom mentions that she's missing $20, but nobody knows where it is. *Doing justice means that you give it to her.*

Because the sinless Savior died, my sinful soul is counted free;
For God, the Just, is satisfied to look on Him and pardon me.

— Charitie Bancroft, 1863 "Before the Throne of God Above"

Lesson 20: Gentleness

Opening activity: Give 3 or 4 children different amounts of uncooked spaghetti: 1, 5, 20, and 100 or so pieces. Have them GENTLY break their pasta. *Make the point that the strength required to be "gentle" varies with the situation.*

Memory verse: Galatians 5:22-23 "the fruit of the Spirit is…gentleness."

Definition: Gentleness is using only the strength or force that is appropriate.

Discussion: How much strength should you use to:

- pet a kitty? *Have them demonstrate.*
- kill a fly or spider?
- close the bedroom door where someone is sleeping? How much is too much?
- swing the bat in T-ball or baseball?
- tag your sister? How much is too much?

Can you remember times you should have been more gentle

- with a brother or sister?
- handling fragile things?
- talking to someone?
- closing doors?

Can you think of times you wish someone had been more gentle with you

- in the way they talked to you?
- in the way they played with you?

Role play: Have small groups of children demonstrate gentleness. Here are some examples to get started.

- Your little sister or brother is bothering you during your play date with a friend your own age. She starts whining and complaining, and you have to take her to your mom to get help. You're very annoyed with her. Demonstrate gentleness in what you say to your sister, how you take her to your mom, and how you explain the problem to your mom.

- A person on your soccer team has a complaining attitude and blames you every time the other team scores or gets the ball. It's not fair, but you know you should have self-control and not return evil for evil. Demonstrate how you can be gentle in your words, tone, and actions.

- You're playing kickball with 20 other children, and some of them are much younger than you are. How do you show gentleness? (Hint: it's okay to be more forceful with older kids, as long as you're gentle with younger kids.)

Take my yoke upon you and learn from me,
for I am gentle and humble in heart,
and you will find rest for your souls.
—Matthew 11:29

Lesson 21: Humility

Opening activity: Choose one child to pretend to be an infant, and choose other students to be parents & siblings. Have the "family" talk about all the things the family has to do to care for the infant. The "baby" can only laugh, whimper, cry, whimper, kick, wave, etc., but not get food, move around, talk to explain a need, etc.

Ask the children if they would like to be helpless, unable to do things for themselves. Consider what it was like for Jesus to become a baby! He gave up his "right" to act like God in order to show us love.

Memory verse: Philippians 2:3 "In humility consider others better than yourselves."

Discuss the picture of the mother and baby: Jesus humbled himself by becoming a man, born as a baby. Spiritually, apart from Christ, you are as helpless as a newborn baby.

Definition: Humility is knowing that everything good in me is from God alone, and is not for my benefit first, but for serving God and others. I shouldn't put myself first.

Discussion: How do we respond when we think we're being treated unfairly? How about these situations? *The teacher should lead this role playing of scenarios that seem unfair. After the discussion, explain the apparent unfairness.*

- At snack time, 3 children get ice cream & cookies, but 1 child gets only soda crackers & water. *The 4th child has been sick and can't eat much yet.*

- Mom gives a new toy/game/outfit to one child, but not to the other. *It was to replace a birthday gift the dog chewed up!*

- Mom and Dad take one child out for lunch, but the

others have to stay home with a babysitter. *Mom and Dad have to tell him about an operation he is going to have.*

Question: Is it important for things to be fair? Why?

Do you ever say:

- It's MY turn!
- ME first! I had my hand up first!!!
- That's not FAIR, he got to go last time!
- But I want it!!

Who is responsible to make sure things are fair? *The one in authority; ultimately, God.*

What are we responsible to do? *Put others first.*

When you're upset because something is unfair, ask yourself: Was it fair for Jesus to be punished because I disobeyed, or because I was unkind to my little brother? Was it fair that Jesus didn't even have his own house to live in?

Why does it matter so much when we're treated unfairly? *Because we put ourselves first. We consider ourselves more important than others, and we don't think how we can serve someone else by giving up our "rights." If we want to be like Jesus, we will consider others more important than ourselves!*

"Your attitude should be the same as that of Jesus Christ: Who, being in very nature God, did not consider equality with God something to be grasped, but made himself nothing, taking the very nature of a servant, being made in human likeness. And being found in appearance as a man, **he humbled himself and became obedient to death—even death on a cross.**"
—Philippianns 2:5-8

Lesson 22: Courage

Opening activity: Ask the children which would be the scariest for them:

- giving a speech in front of the whole church

- killing a snake

- climbing onto the roof of the house

- being left alone in your house at night

- being outside in a big lightning & thunder storm

Then, help them think of good reasons why they might need to do each of those things. Ask them, "How could you ever do something you are too scared to do? That takes COURAGE!" And that is what today's lesson is about.

Memory verse: Joshua 1:9 "Be strong and courageous. Do not be terrified; do not be discouraged, for the Lord your God will be with you wherever you go."

Definition: Courage is doing what must be done, even when I am afraid and I think it is too hard.

Discussion: Is it courageous to:

- Jump out of a second-story window because you're supposed to stay in your room until you finish cleaning it, and you want to go out and play? *No, that's disobedience and foolishness.*

- Jump out of a second story window because the house is on fire and your daddy tells you to jump and he'll catch you? *Yes, that's obeying when it's hard.*

- Crawl across a field where people are firing guns for target practice? *No, that's dangerous and foolish, because there's no good reason to take the risk.*

- Crawl across a field in a battle to rescue someone who has been injured? *Yes, that's courageous, because you are considering someone else more important than yourself.*

- Tell your teacher she is wrong when you think she made a mistake? *No, that's being disrespectful of authority.*

- Answer a question in school by saying that God created the world, and Jesus is God—when the teacher said that there is no God and Jesus was only a good man? *Yes, that is honoring God rather than man, even when you might suffer for Christ's sake.*

How can you be brave and courageous when you have to do something really hard?

Remember what the Lord said to Joshua: don't be afraid because the Lord your God will be with you wherever you go. When you need courage, pray and ask God to help you do the hard thing because you love him and want to please him. He will help you.

Role play: Have the children act out the following scenes.

- You and your friend accidentally get seperated from your group at a big amusement park. There is a massive lightning storm and heavy rain, and you are terrified of the thunder. What do you do?

- A teacher says that children should make decisions for themselves, not just believe their parents—especially about religion. Then she asks if you believe what your parents have taught you about God. What do you say?

Be on your guard; stand firm in the faith; be men of courage; be strong. Do everything in love. —1 Corinthians 16:13-14

Lesson 23: Love

Opening activity: Ask the students:

Whom do you love? *Parents? Siblings? Friends? Teachers? Grandparents? Cousins?*

What things do you love? *Pets? Toys? Movies? Music?*

What is love? *Introduce memory verse.*

Memory verse: John 13:34 "As I have loved you, so you must love one another."

What does Jesus mean? How does he want us to love one another?

Definition: Love is giving willingly of whatever I have to meet someone else's need.

Discussion: How did Jesus love people? How did he meet their needs?

- *He healed people.*
- *He fed people.*
- *He taught people.*
- *He explained people's problems and forgave their sin.*

Do you think it was ever hard for Jesus to love people? *Yes, sometimes he was tired and hungry, and sometimes people were unkind and mean to him, but he always responded the right way, even when it was hard.*

Can you think of any other Bible verses about love? *Direct if necessary. Especially see if they will think of:*

Matthew 22:37–40, "Jesus replied, 'Love the Lord your God with all your heart and with all your soul and with all your mind.' This is the first and greatest commandment. And the second is like it: 'Love your neigh–

bor as yourself.' All the Law and the Prophets hang on these two commandments."

The Bible says you should love your neighbor as yourself. How do you love yourself when:

- You fall down and scrape your knee and it's bleeding? *You take care of it carefully.*

- Mom makes your favorite dessert. *Eat as much as possible!*

- You have a whole afternoon of free time. *You do whatever YOU want to do.*

How could you love your neighbor as yourself when:

- He hurts himself? *Help him get it taken care of.*
- Mom makes your favorite dessert? *Share with her.*
- You have free time? *Think of how to make a great afternoon for someone else—maybe your little brother and sister.*

Role play: Have the children act out how to love their neighbors as themselves in these situations.

- Your class is going on a long field trip, and you want to ride with your friends, but there's only one seat left in their van, and you see that a shy girl who is just starting to make friends needs a seat. What will you do?

- You love sports and you're always a team leader during recess. There's one boy who tries to play, but he's clumsy and he doesn't even know the rules. How can you love this neighbor as yourself?

In this is love, not that we have loved God but that he loved us and sent his Son to be the propitiation for our sins. —1 John 4:10 (ESV)